GRAPHIC LIBRARY™

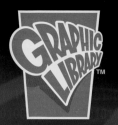

GRAPHIC SCIENCE

THE SHOCKING WORLD OF ELECTRICITY WITH MAX AXIOM SUPER SCIENTIST

by Liam O'Donnell
illustrated by Richard Dominguez
and Charles Barnett III

Consultant:
Dr. Ronald Browne
Associate Professor of Elementary Education
Minnesota State University, Mankato

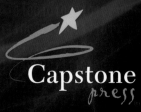

Capstone press
Mankato, Minnesota

Graphic Library is published by Capstone Press,
1710 Roe Crest Drive, North Mankato, Minnesota 56003.
www.capstonepub.com

 Books published by Capstone Press are manufactured with paper
containing at least 10 percent post-consumer waste.

Library of Congress Cataloging-in-Publication Data
O'Donnell, Liam, 1970–
    The shocking world of electricity with Max Axiom, super scientist / by Liam O'Donnell;
illustrated by Richard Dominguez and Charles Barnett III.
    p. cm.—(Graphic library. graphic science)
    Includes bibliographical references and index.
    ISBN-13: 978-0-7368-6835-8 (hardcover)
    ISBN-10: 0-7368-6835-6 (harcover)
    ISBN-13: 978-0-7368-7888-3 (softcover pbk.)
    ISBN-10: 0-7368-7888-2 (softcover pbk.)
    1. Electricity—Juvenile literature. 2. Adventure stories—Juvenile literature. I. Title.
II. Series.
QC527.2.O44 2007
537—dc22   2006029237

Summary: In graphic novel format, follows the adventures of Max Axiom as he explains the
science behind electricity.

Art Director and Designer
Bob Lentz

Colorists
Ben Hunzeker and Kim Brown

Cover Artist
Tod Smith

Editor
Donald Lemke

Printed in the United States of America in Stevens Point, Wisconsin.
062014   008307R

TABLE OF CONTENTS

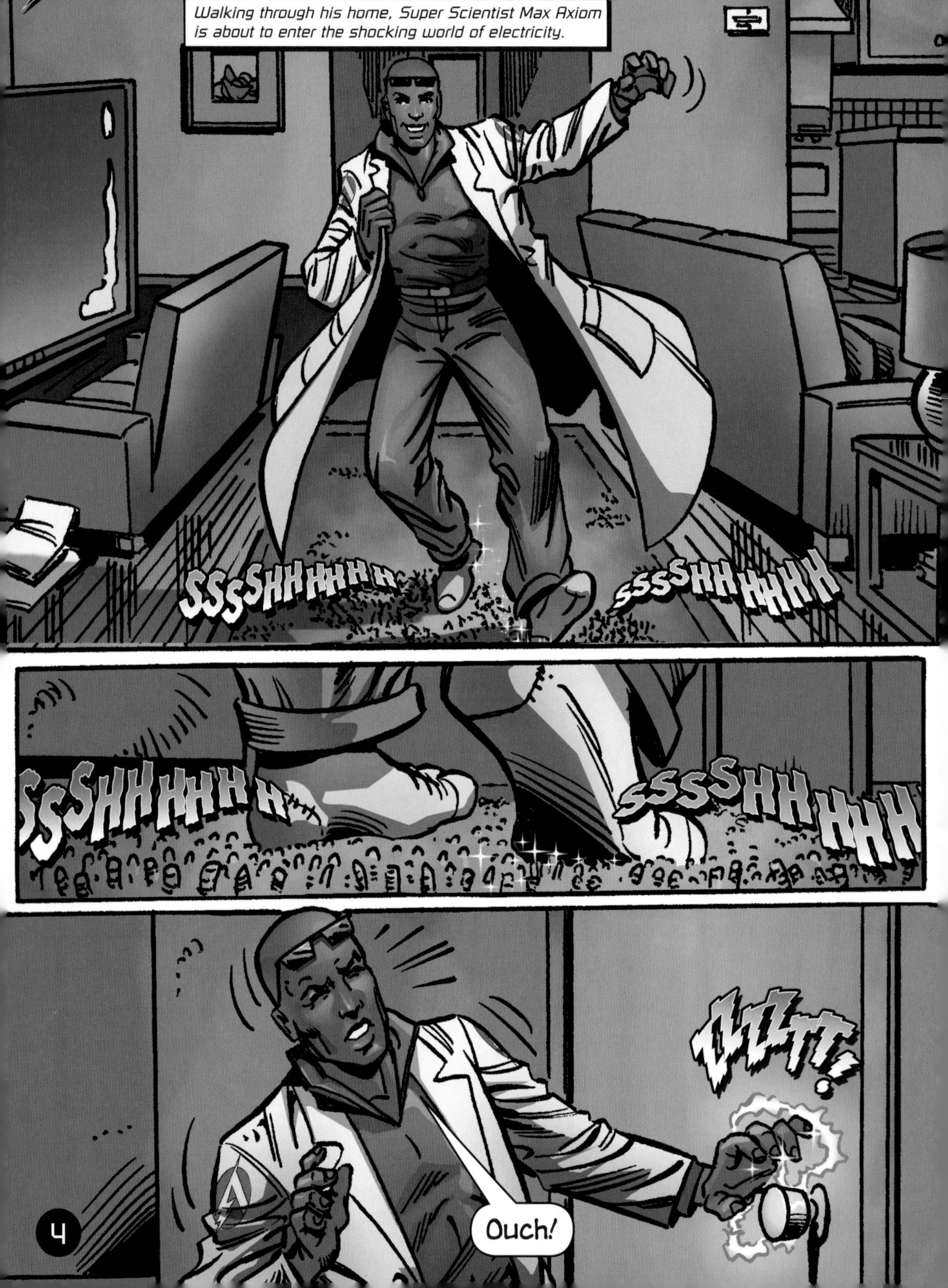
Walking through his home, Super Scientist Max Axiom is about to enter the shocking world of electricity.
SSSSHHHHHHH
SSSSHHHHHHH
SSSHHHHHH
SSSSHHHHH
ZZZZTT!
Ouch!

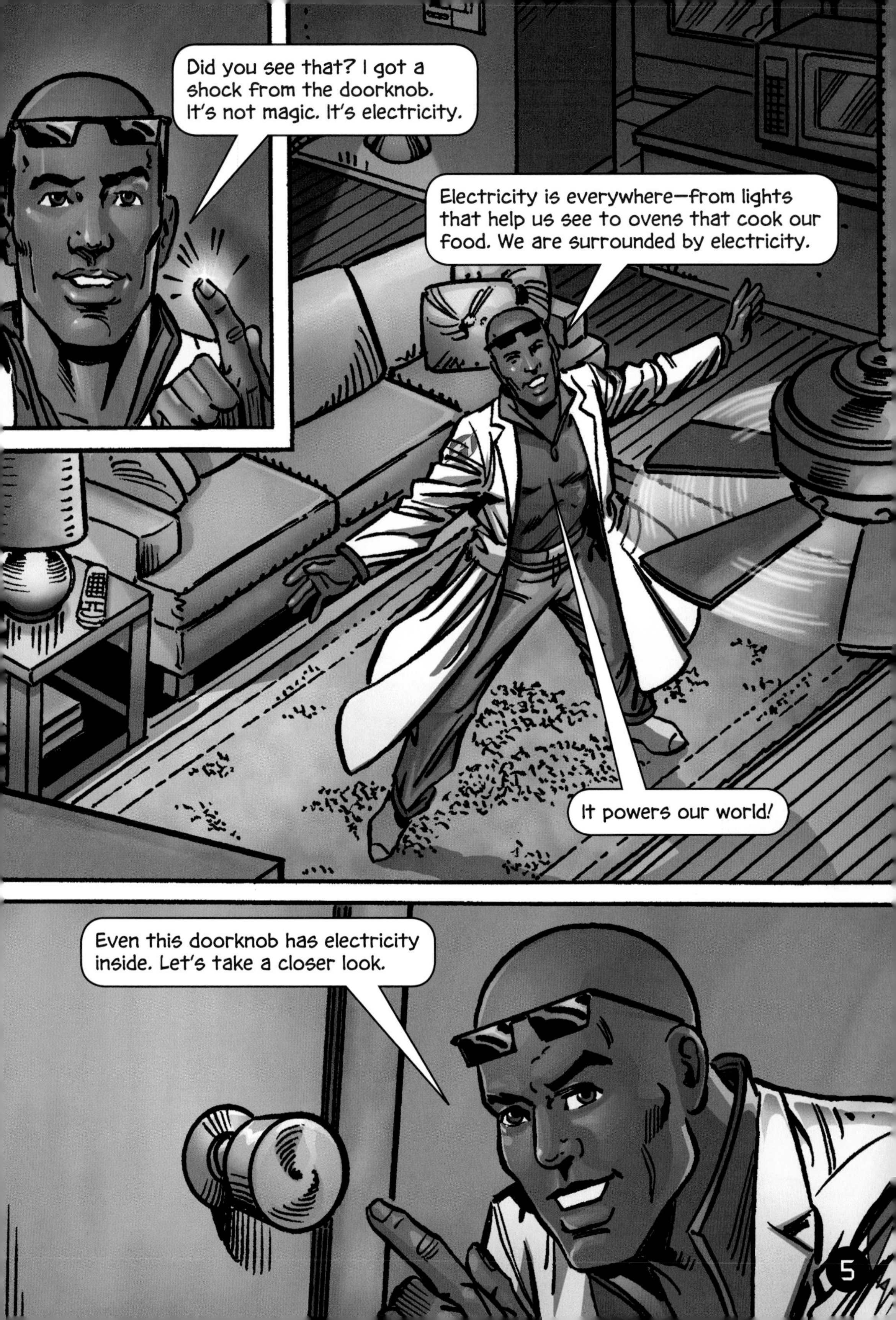

Did you see that? I got a shock from the doorknob. It's not magic. It's electricity.
Electricity is everywhere—from lights that help us see to ovens that cook our food. We are surrounded by electricity.
It powers our world!
Even this doorknob has electricity inside. Let's take a closer look.

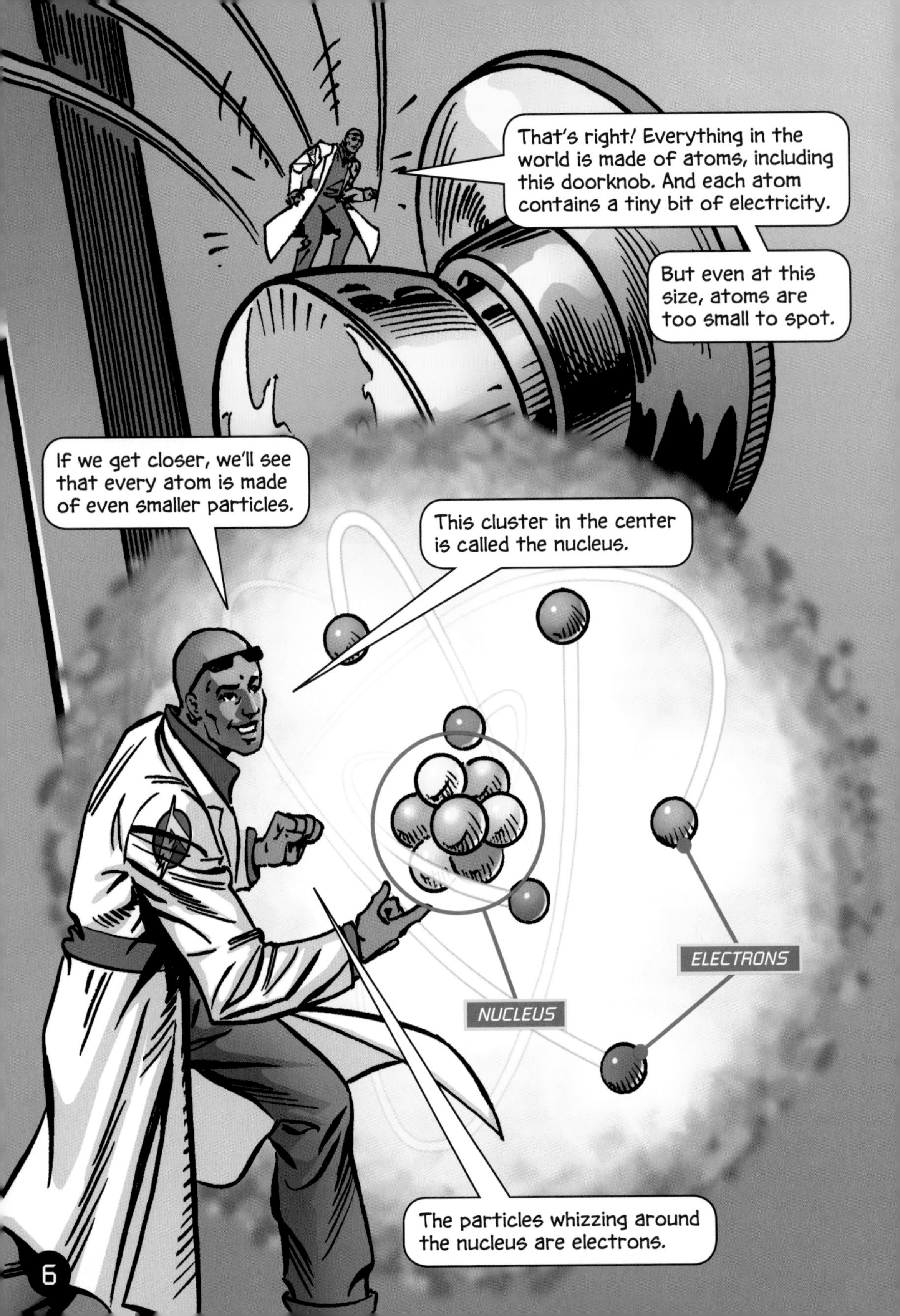
That's right! Everything in the world is made of atoms, including this doorknob. And each atom contains a tiny bit of electricity.
But even at this size, atoms are too small to spot.
If we get closer, we'll see that every atom is made of even smaller particles.
This cluster in the center is called the nucleus.
NUCLEUS
ELECTRONS
The particles whizzing around the nucleus are electrons.

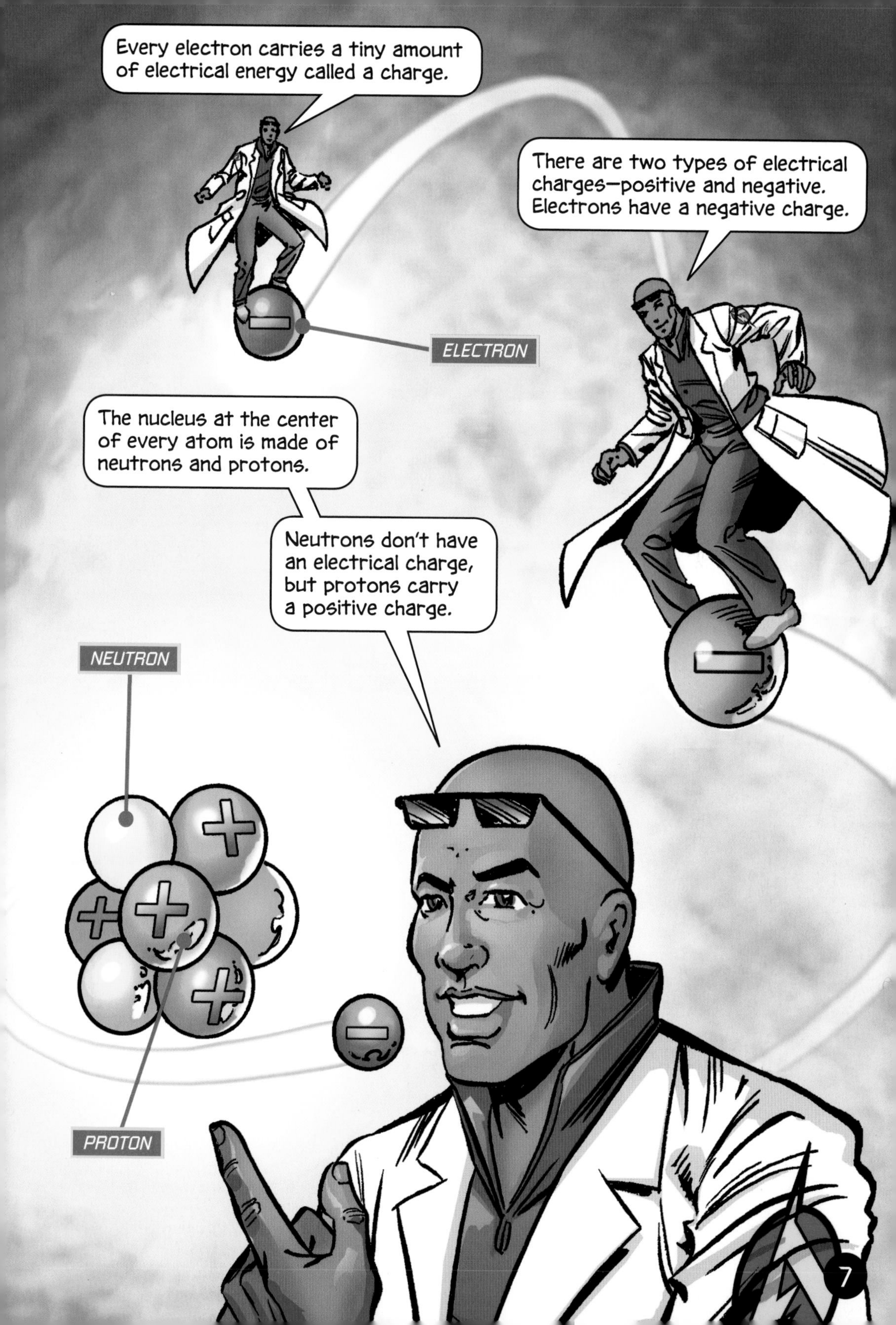
Every electron carries a tiny amount of electrical energy called a charge.
There are two types of electrical charges—positive and negative. Electrons have a negative charge.
ELECTRON
The nucleus at the center of every atom is made of neutrons and protons.
Neutrons don't have an electrical charge, but protons carry a positive charge.
NEUTRON
PROTON

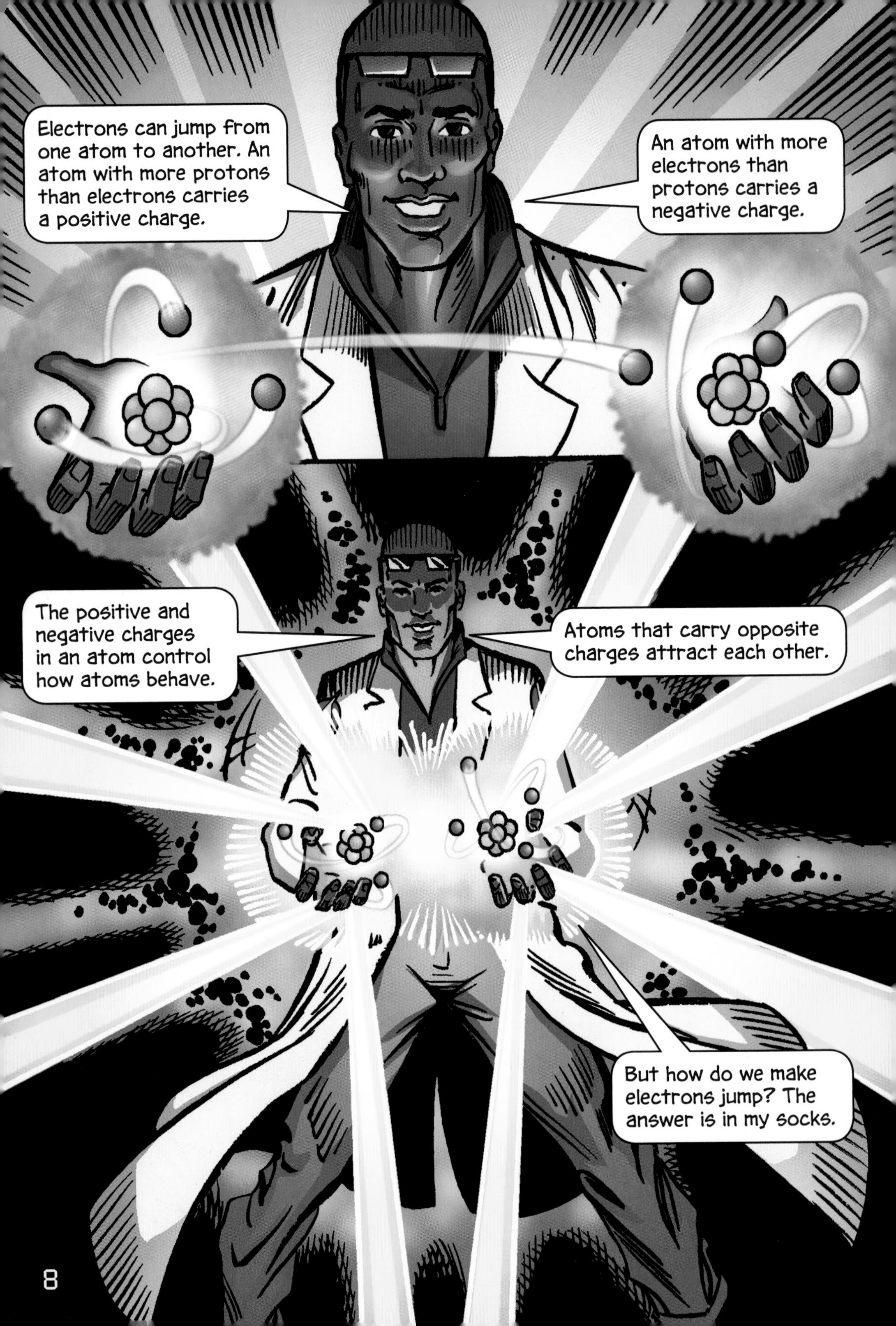
Electrons can jump from one atom to another. An atom with more protons than electrons carries a positive charge.
An atom with more electrons than protons carries a negative charge.
The positive and negative charges in an atom control how atoms behave.
Atoms that carry opposite charges attract each other.
But how do we make electrons jump? The answer is in my socks.

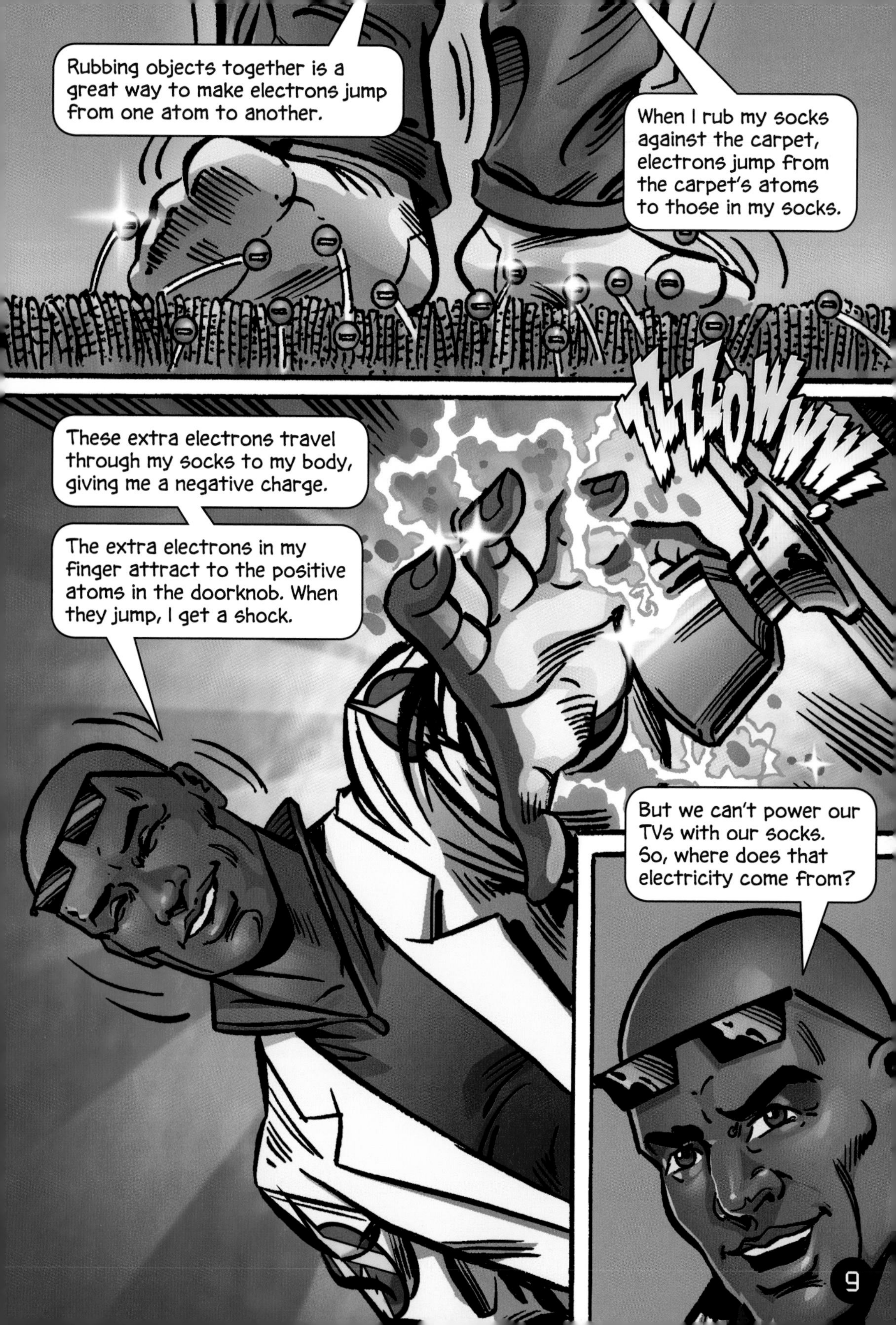

Rubbing objects together is a great way to make electrons jump from one atom to another.
When I rub my socks against the carpet, electrons jump from the carpet's atoms to those in my socks.
ZZZOWWW!
These extra electrons travel through my socks to my body, giving me a negative charge.
The extra electrons in my finger attract to the positive atoms in the doorknob. When they jump, I get a shock.
But we can't power our TVs with our socks. So, where does that electricity come from?

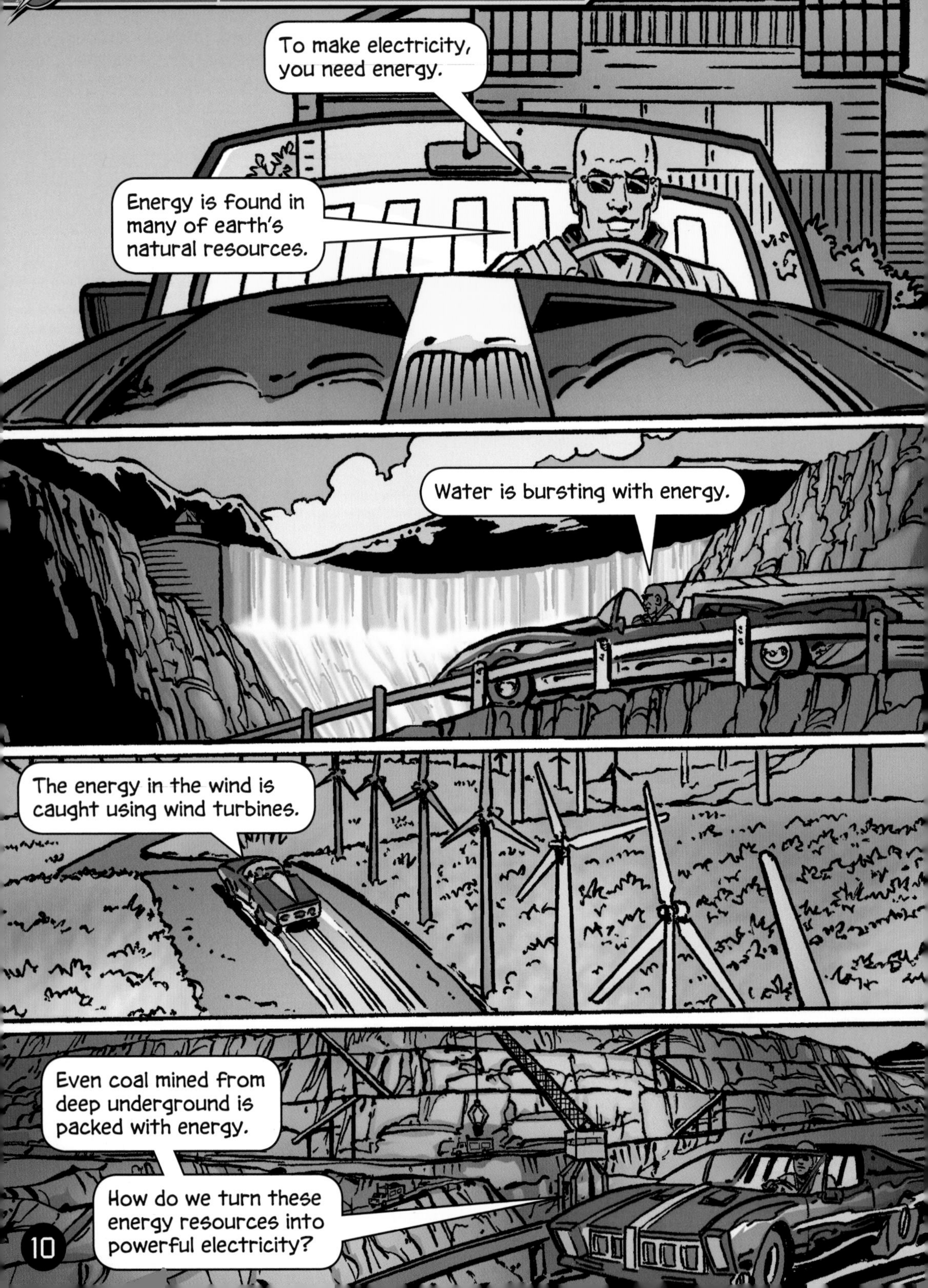
To make electricity, you need energy.
Energy is found in many of earth's natural resources.
Water is bursting with energy.
The energy in the wind is caught using wind turbines.
Even coal mined from deep underground is packed with energy.
How do we turn these energy resources into powerful electricity?

ENERGY SOURCES

Renewable energy is a source that cannot be used up completely. Water in rivers or the heat from the sun are renewable energy sources. Energy from coal and oil can be used up. They are examples of nonrenewable energy.

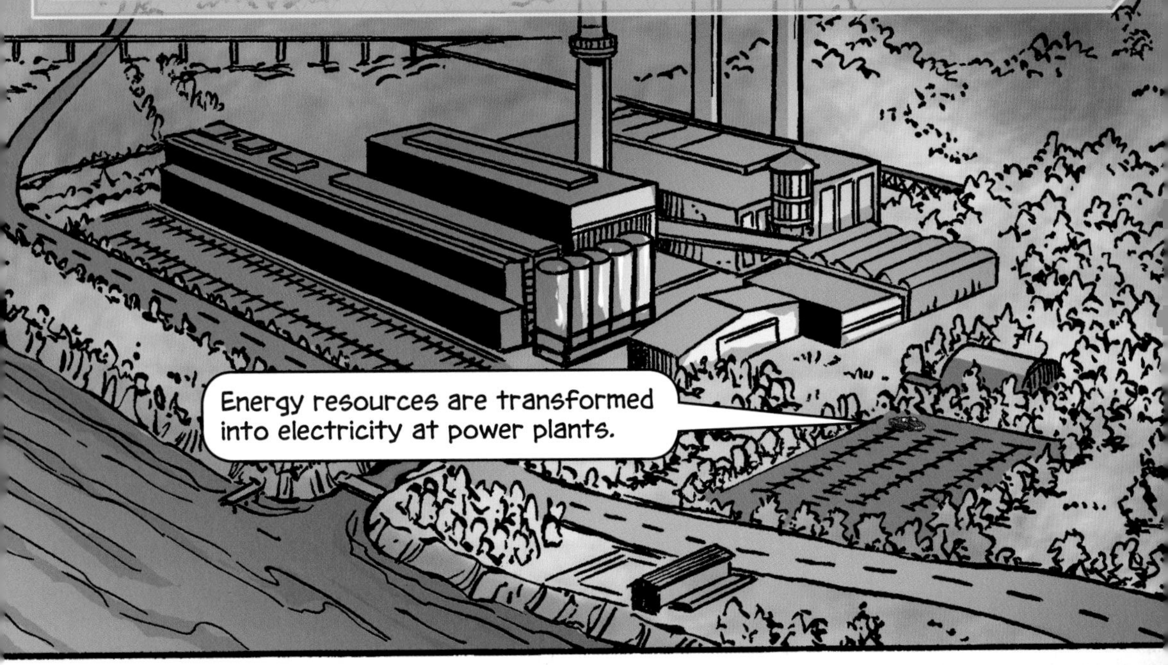

Energy resources are transformed into electricity at power plants.

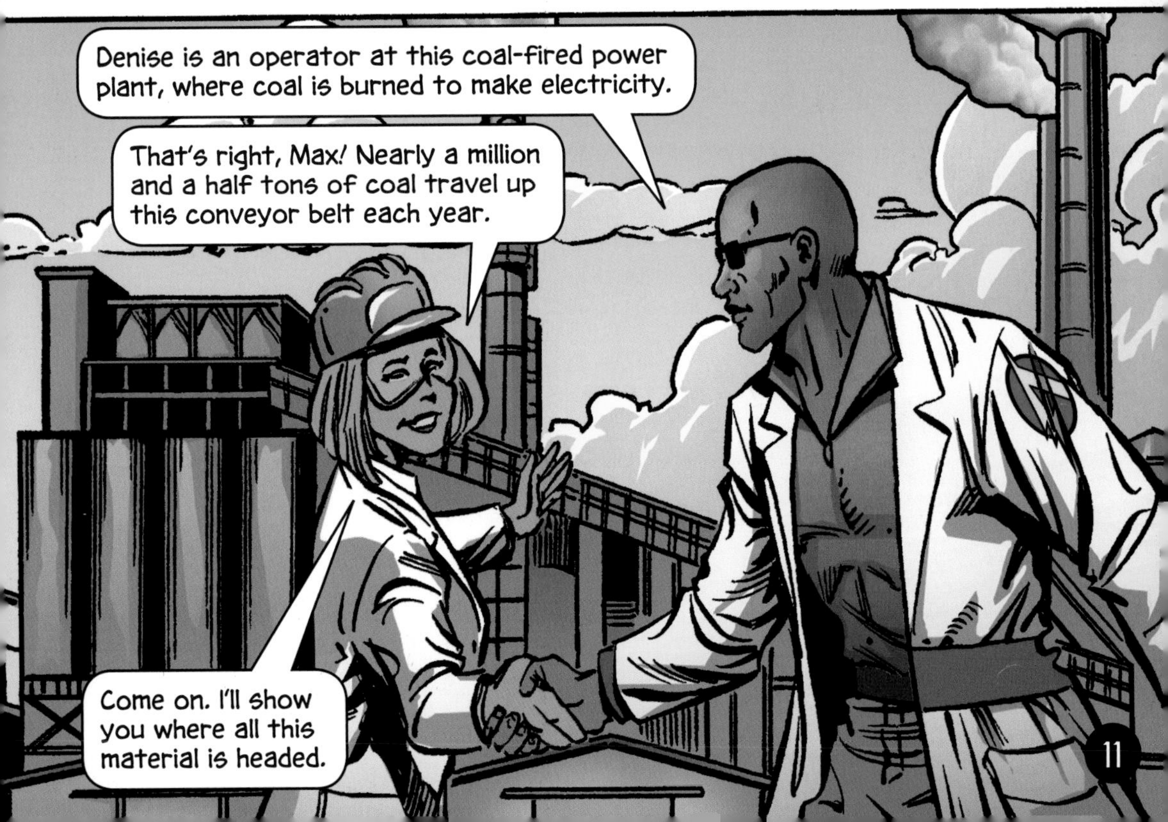

Denise is an operator at this coal-fired power plant, where coal is burned to make electricity.
That's right, Max! Nearly a million and a half tons of coal travel up this conveyor belt each year.
Come on. I'll show you where all this material is headed.

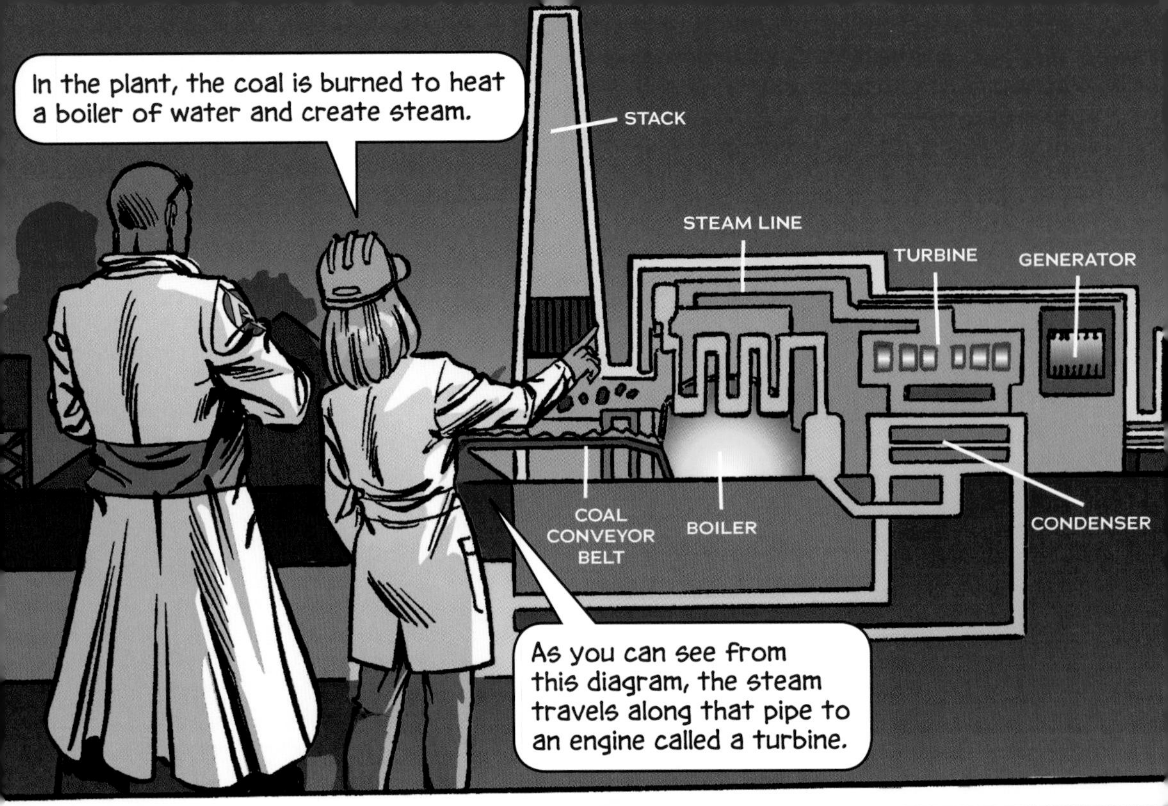
In the plant, the coal is burned to heat a boiler of water and create steam.
STACK
STEAM LINE
TURBINE
GENERATOR
COAL CONVEYOR BELT
BOILER
CONDENSER
As you can see from this diagram, the steam travels along that pipe to an engine called a turbine.

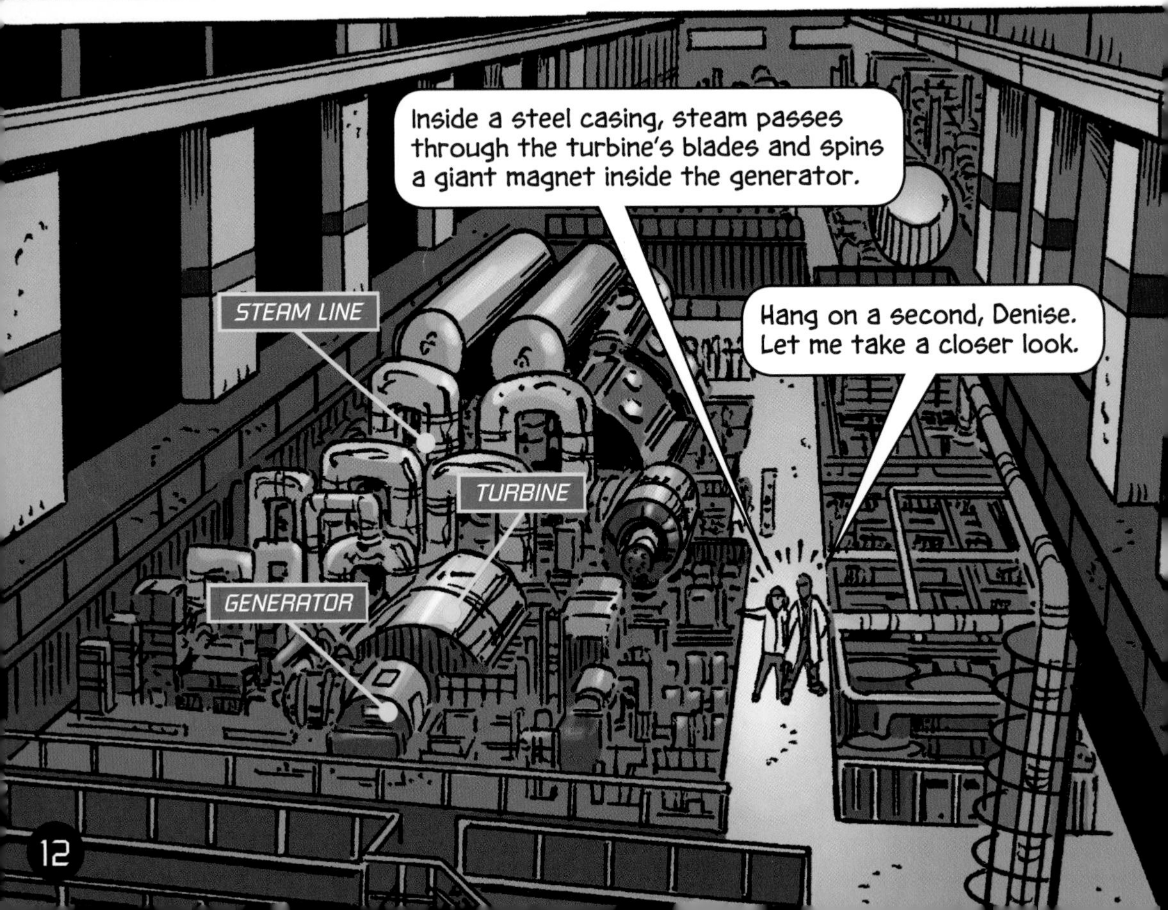
Inside a steel casing, steam passes through the turbine's blades and spins a giant magnet inside the generator.
STEAM LINE
TURBINE
GENERATOR
Hang on a second, Denise. Let me take a closer look.

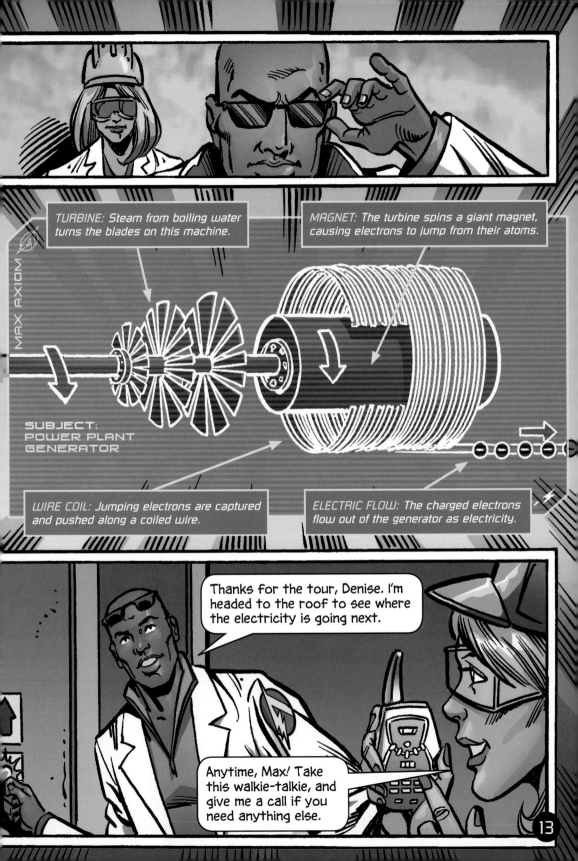

MAX AXIOM

TURBINE: Steam from boiling water turns the blades on this machine.

MAGNET: The turbine spins a giant magnet, causing electrons to jump from their atoms.

SUBJECT:
POWER PLANT
GENERATOR

WIRE COIL: Jumping electrons are captured and pushed along a coiled wire.

ELECTRIC FLOW: The charged electrons flow out of the generator as electricity.

Thanks for the tour, Denise. I'm headed to the roof to see where the electricity is going next.

Anytime, Max! Take this walkie-talkie, and give me a call if you need anything else.

13

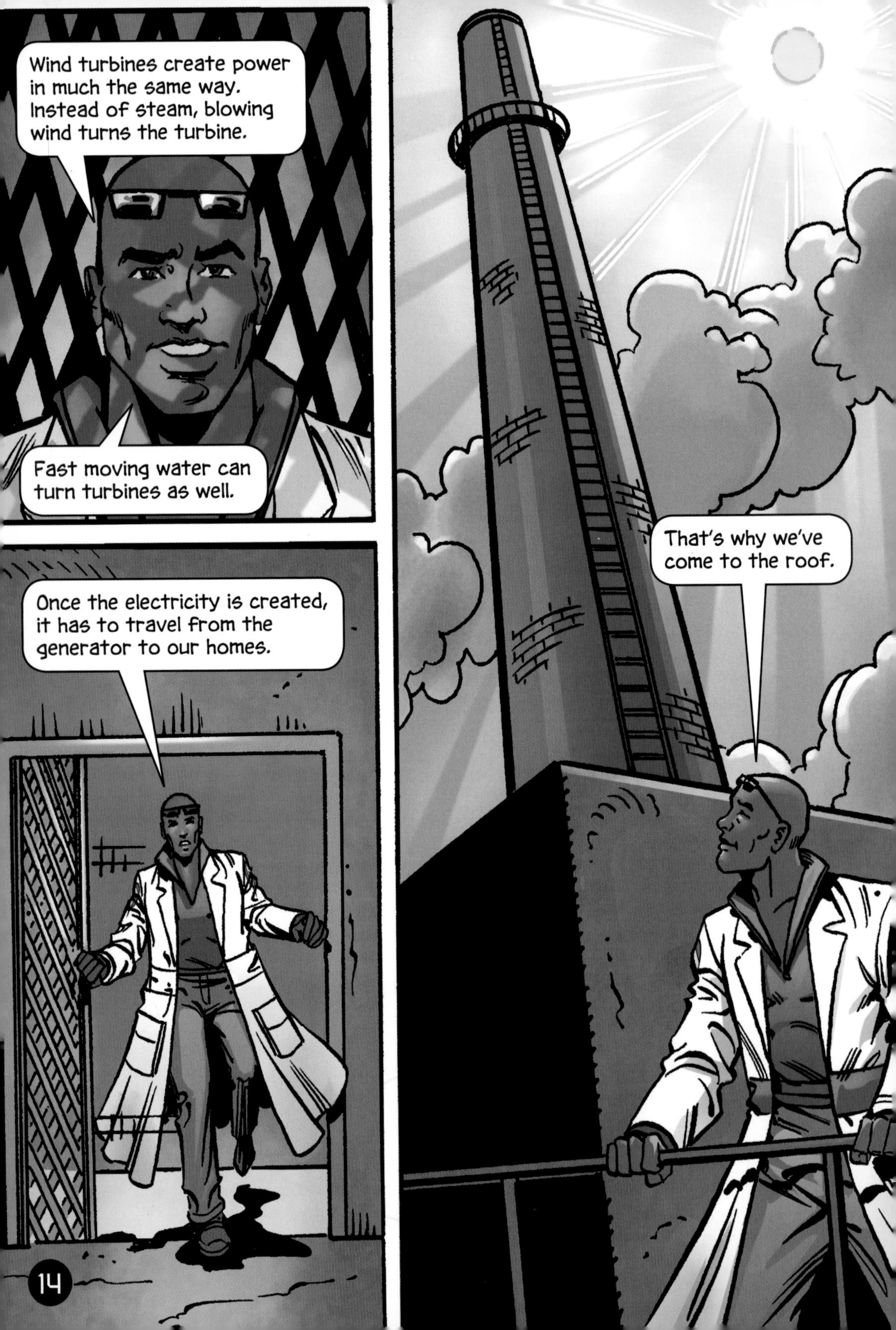

Wind turbines create power in much the same way. Instead of steam, blowing wind turns the turbine.
Fast moving water can turn turbines as well.
Once the electricity is created, it has to travel from the generator to our homes.
That's why we've come to the roof.

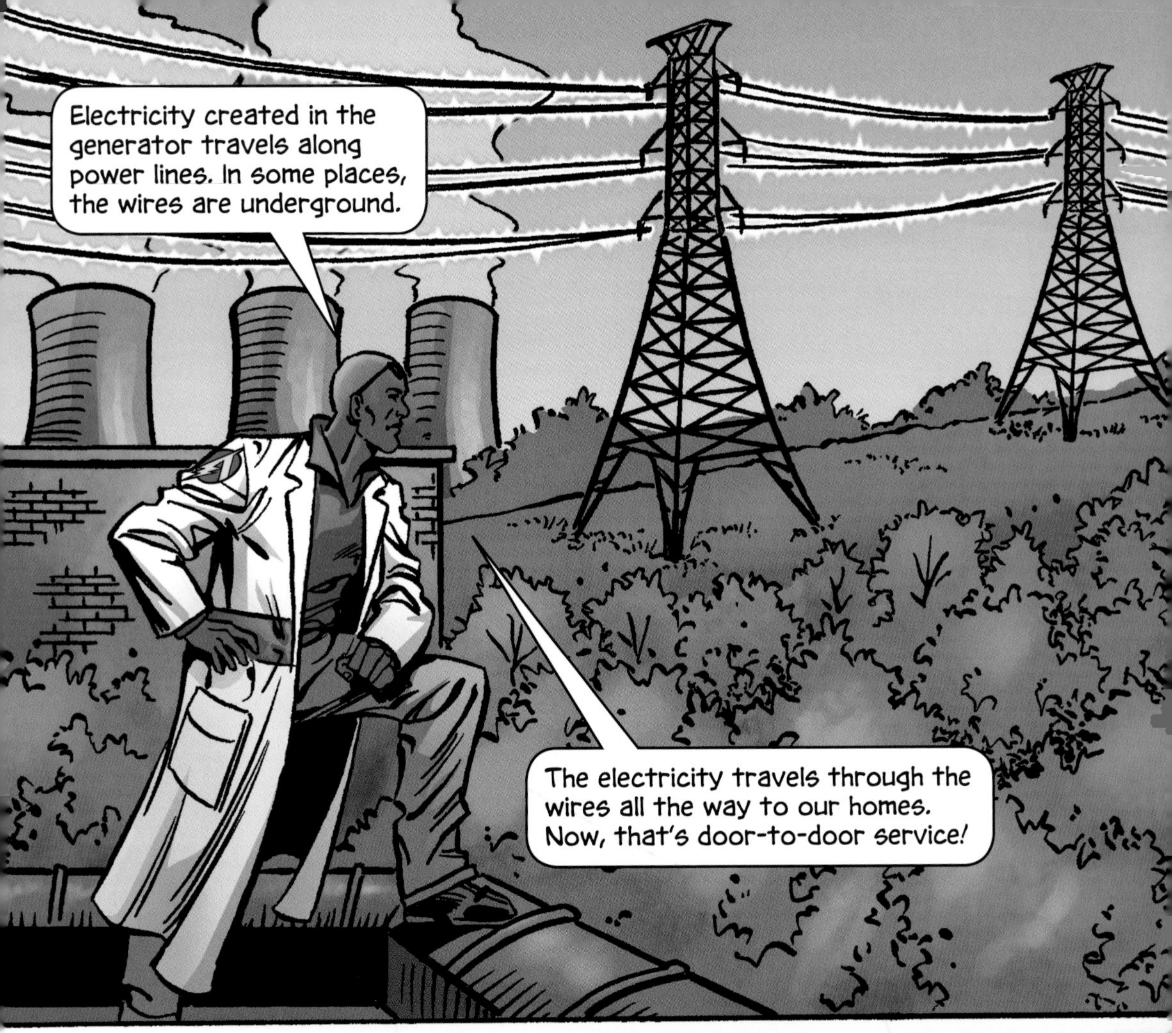
Electricity created in the generator travels along power lines. In some places, the wires are underground.
The electricity travels through the wires all the way to our homes. Now, that's door-to-door service!

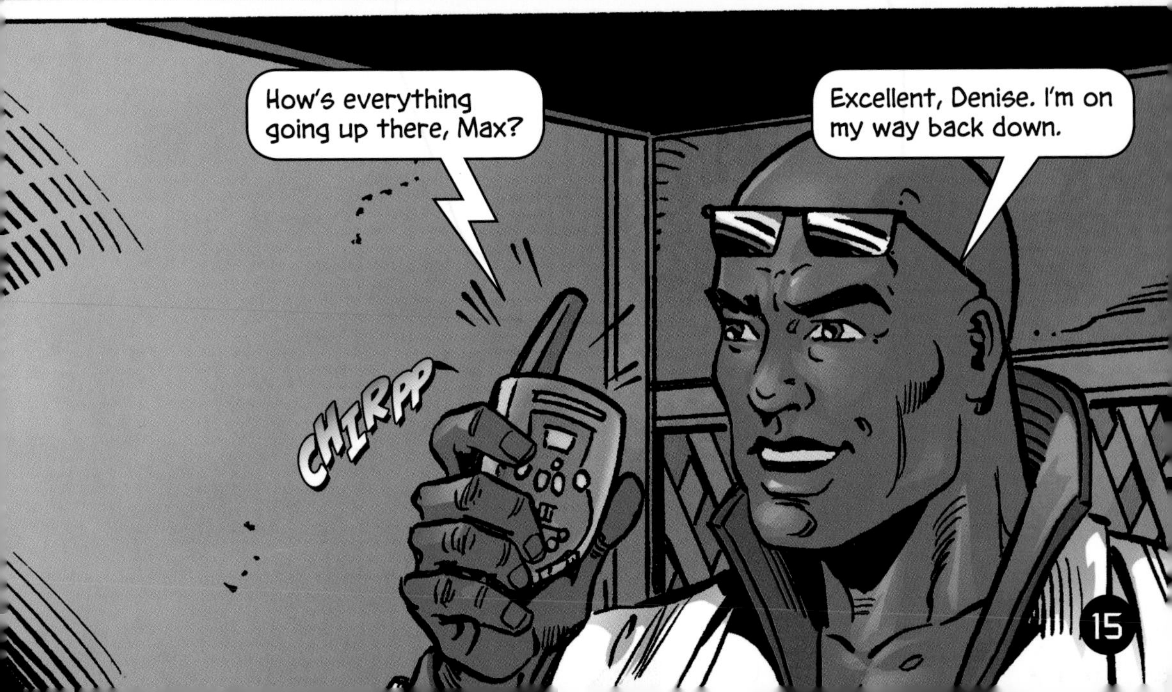
How's everything going up there, Max?
CHIRPP
Excellent, Denise. I'm on my way back down.

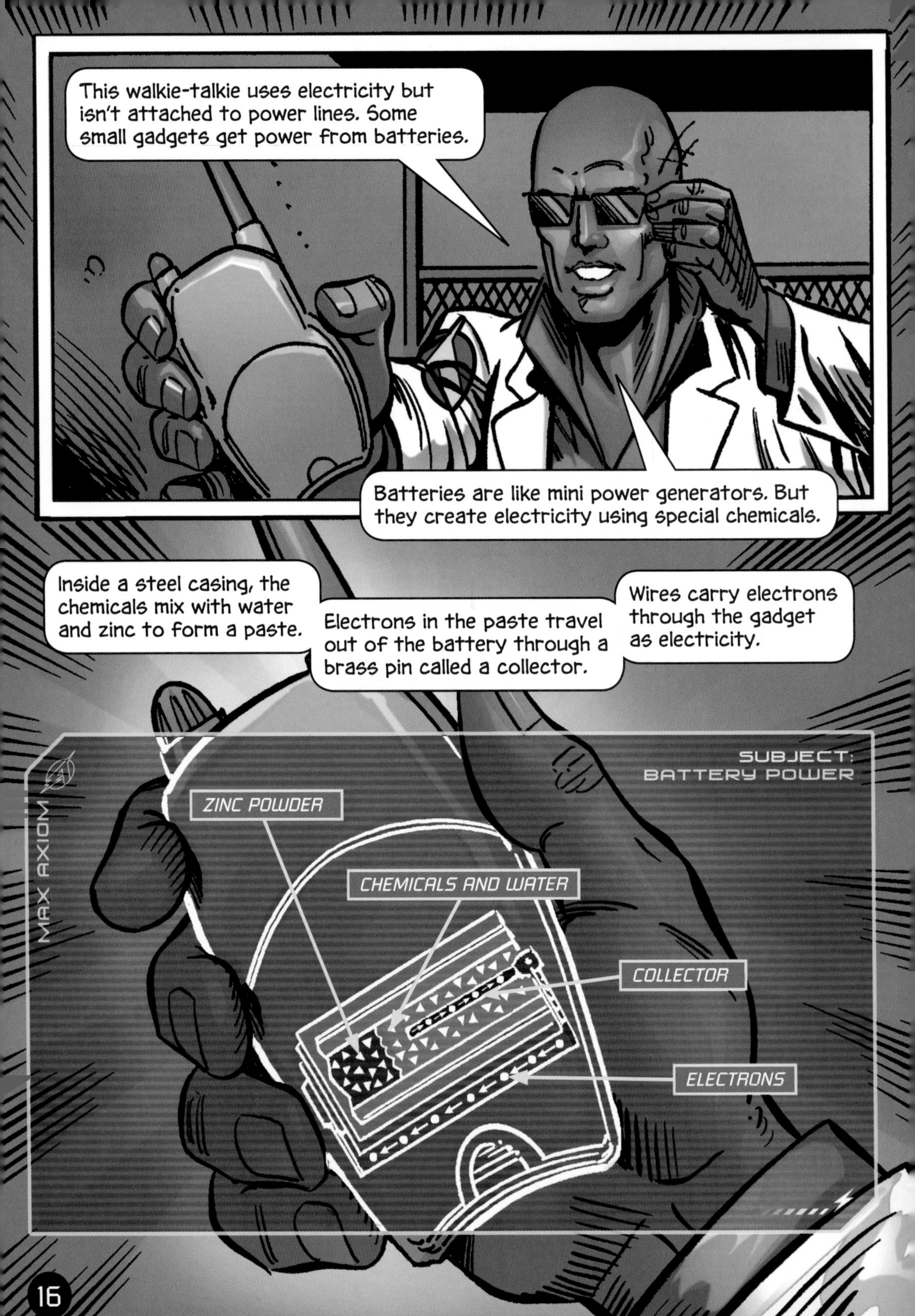
This walkie-talkie uses electricity but isn't attached to power lines. Some small gadgets get power from batteries.
Batteries are like mini power generators. But they create electricity using special chemicals.
Inside a steel casing, the chemicals mix with water and zinc to form a paste.
Electrons in the paste travel out of the battery through a brass pin called a collector.
Wires carry electrons through the gadget as electricity.
MAX AXIOM
SUBJECT: BATTERY POWER
ZINC POWDER
CHEMICALS AND WATER
COLLECTOR
ELECTRONS

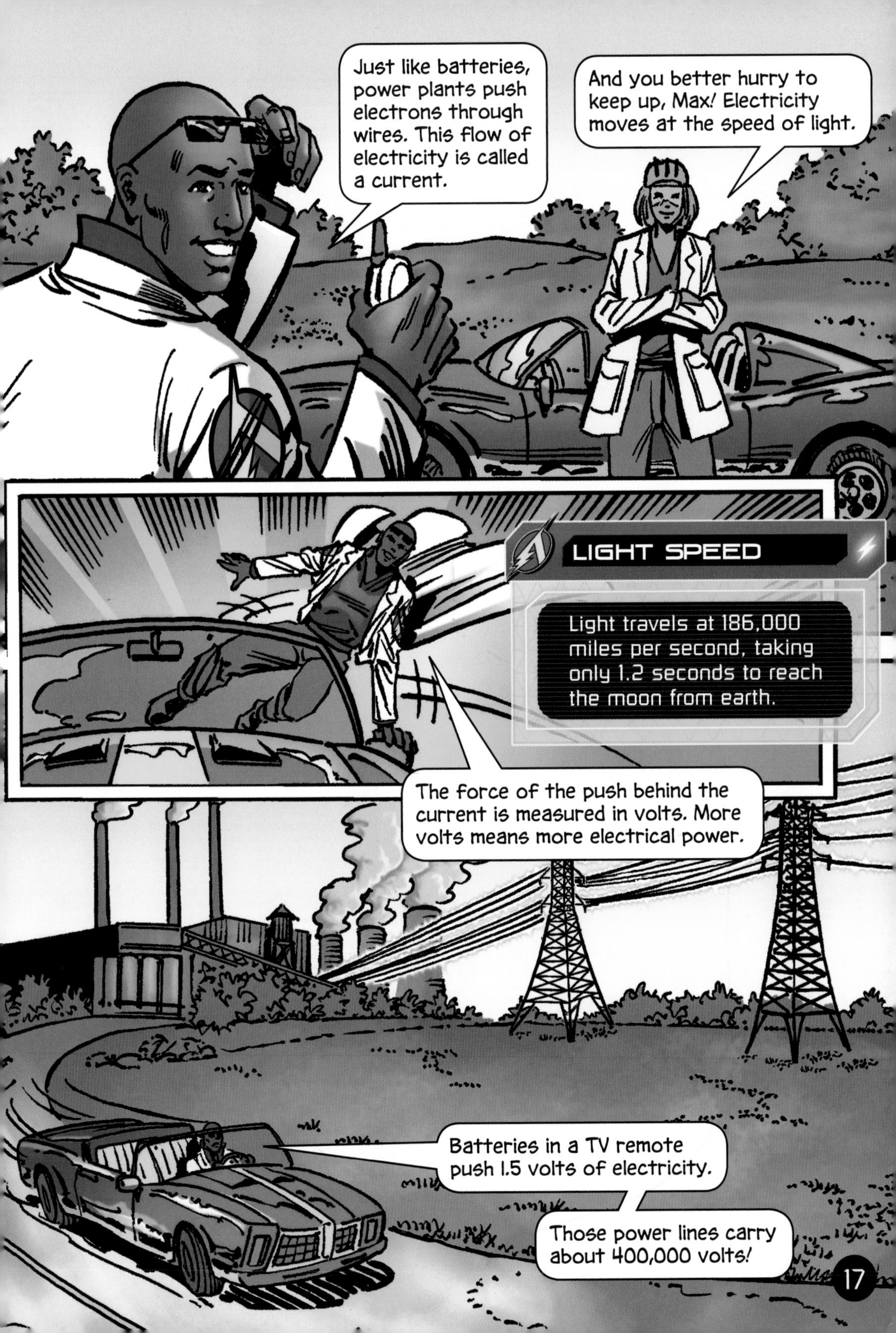

Just like batteries, power plants push electrons through wires. This flow of electricity is called a current.
And you better hurry to keep up, Max! Electricity moves at the speed of light.
LIGHT SPEED
Light travels at 186,000 miles per second, taking only 1.2 seconds to reach the moon from earth.
The force of the push behind the current is measured in volts. More volts means more electrical power.
Batteries in a TV remote push 1.5 volts of electricity.
Those power lines carry about 400,000 volts!

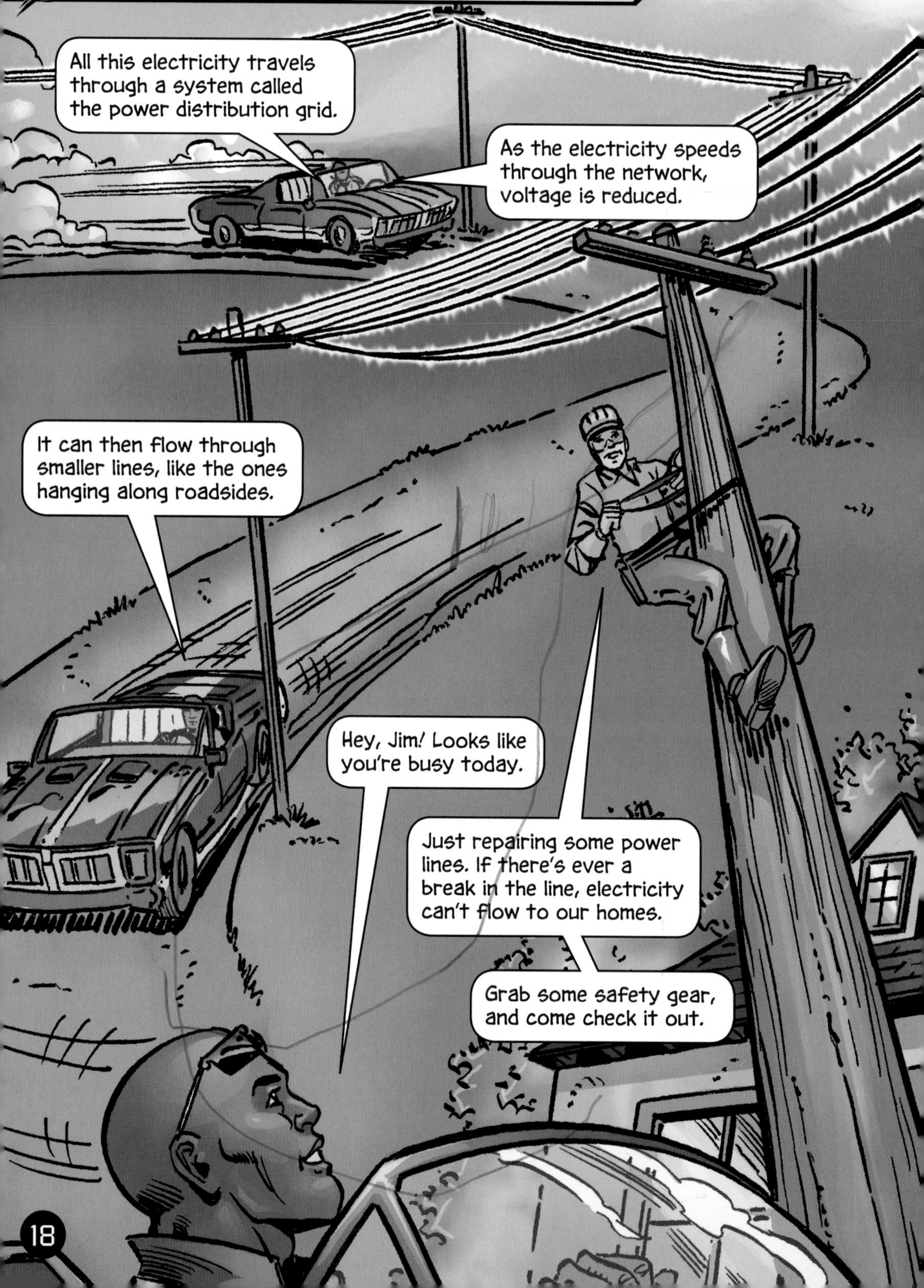
All this electricity travels through a system called the power distribution grid.
As the electricity speeds through the network, voltage is reduced.
It can then flow through smaller lines, like the ones hanging along roadsides.
Hey, Jim! Looks like you're busy today.
Just repairing some power lines. If there's ever a break in the line, electricity can't flow to our homes.
Grab some safety gear, and come check it out.

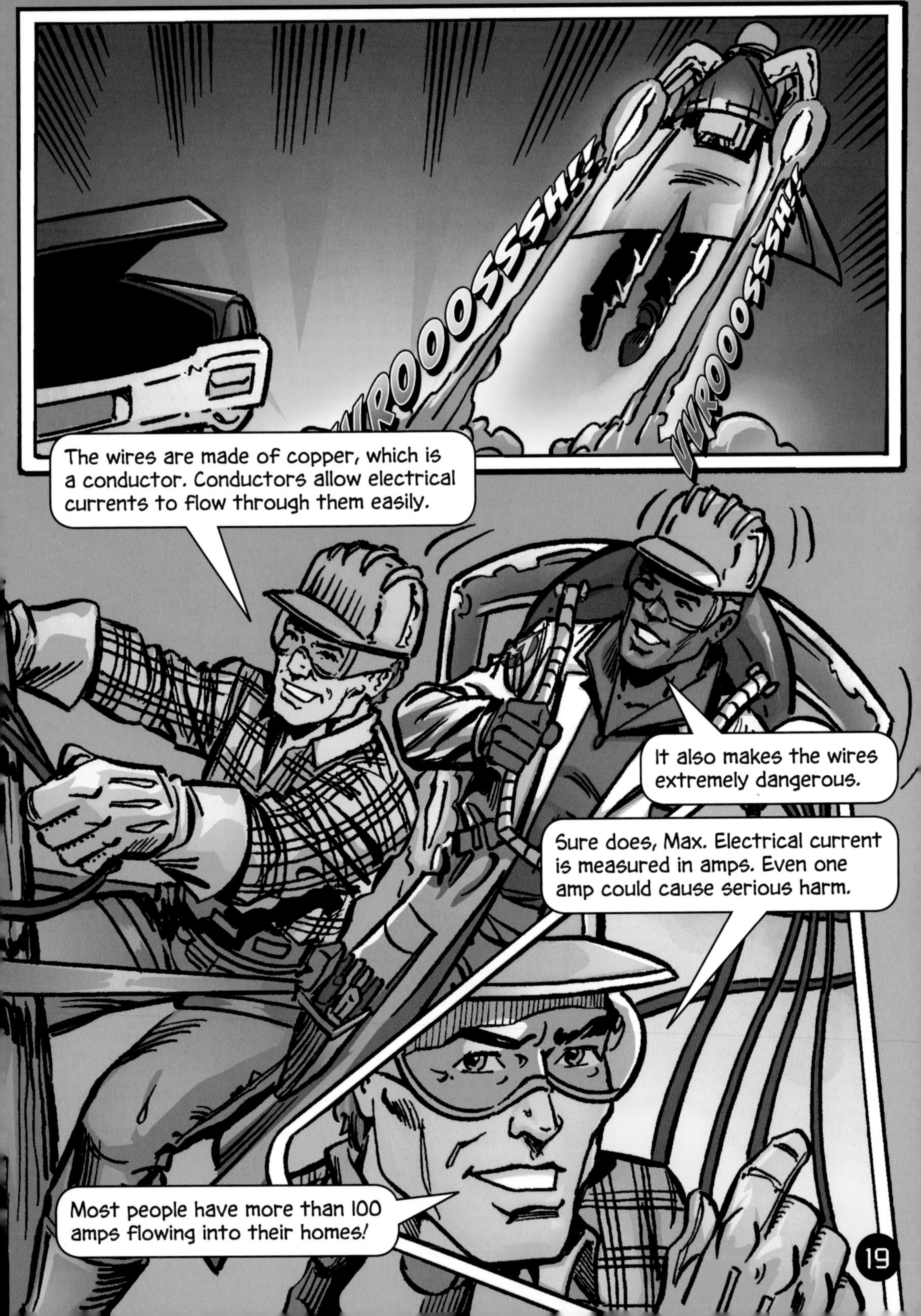
VVROOOSSSSH!!
VVROOOSSSSH!!
The wires are made of copper, which is a conductor. Conductors allow electrical currents to flow through them easily.
It also makes the wires extremely dangerous.
Sure does, Max. Electrical current is measured in amps. Even one amp could cause serious harm.
Most people have more than 100 amps flowing into their homes!

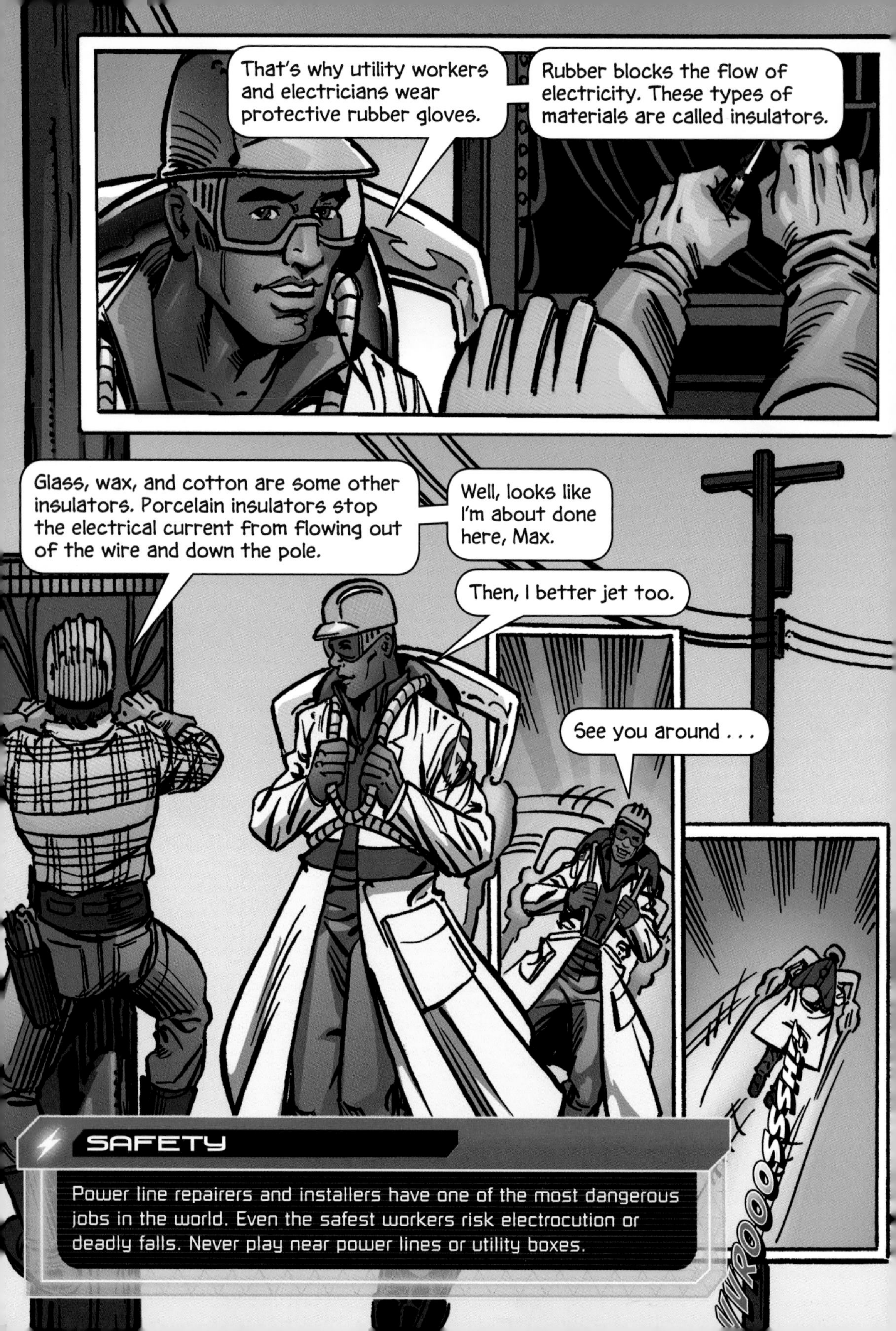
That's why utility workers and electricians wear protective rubber gloves.
Rubber blocks the flow of electricity. These types of materials are called insulators.
Glass, wax, and cotton are some other insulators. Porcelain insulators stop the electrical current from flowing out of the wire and down the pole.
Well, looks like I'm about done here, Max.
Then, I better jet too.
See you around . . .

SAFETY

Power line repairers and installers have one of the most dangerous jobs in the world. Even the safest workers risk electrocution or deadly falls. Never play near power lines or utility boxes.

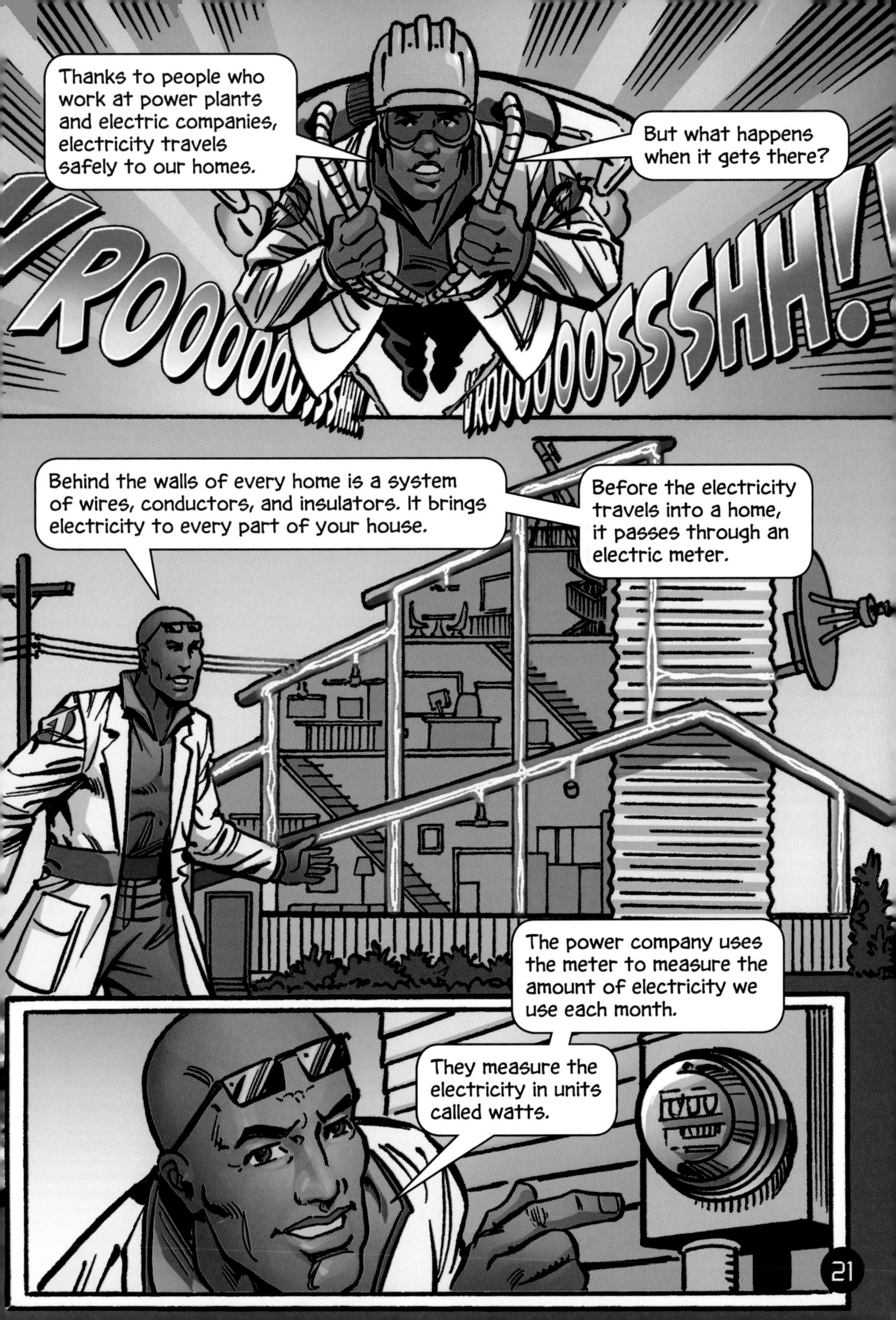
Thanks to people who work at power plants and electric companies, electricity travels safely to our homes.
But what happens when it gets there?
Behind the walls of every home is a system of wires, conductors, and insulators. It brings electricity to every part of your house.
Before the electricity travels into a home, it passes through an electric meter.
The power company uses the meter to measure the amount of electricity we use each month.
They measure the electricity in units called watts.

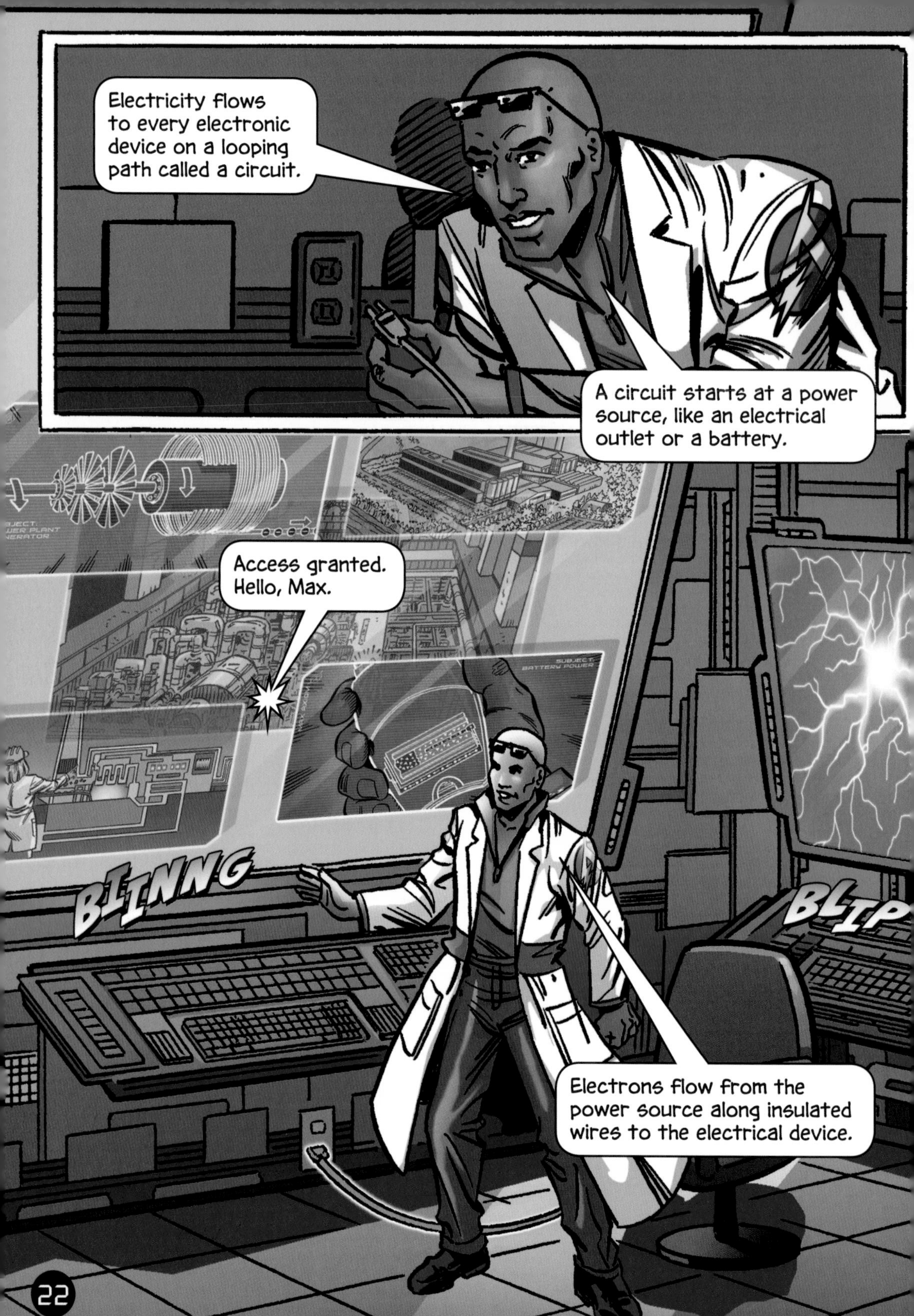
Electricity flows to every electronic device on a looping path called a circuit.
A circuit starts at a power source, like an electrical outlet or a battery.
Access granted. Hello, Max.
BIINNG
BLIP
Electrons flow from the power source along insulated wires to the electrical device.

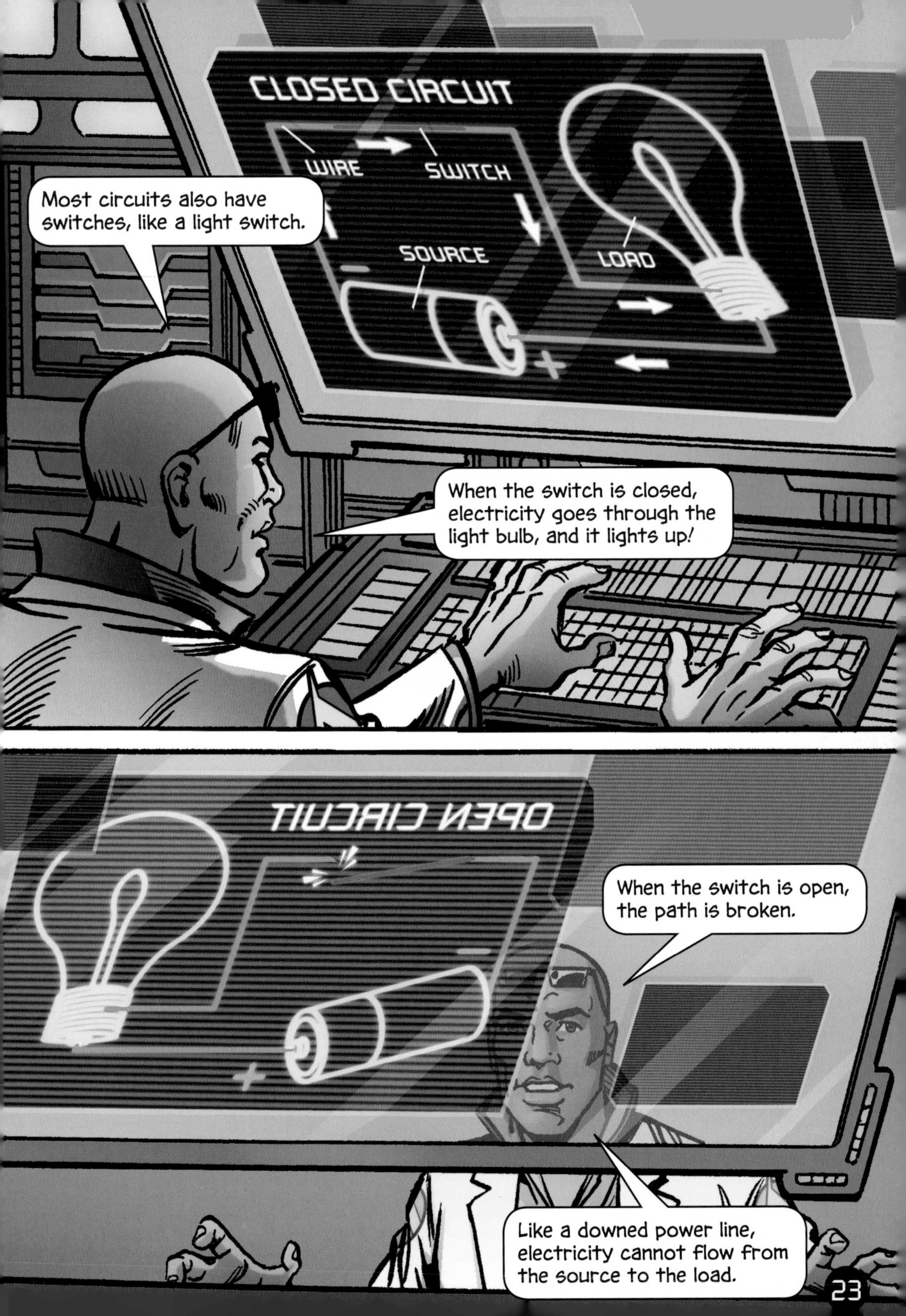
CLOSED CIRCUIT
WIRE
SWITCH
SOURCE
LOAD
Most circuits also have switches, like a light switch.
When the switch is closed, electricity goes through the light bulb, and it lights up!
OPEN CIRCUIT
When the switch is open, the path is broken.
Like a downed power line, electricity cannot flow from the source to the load.

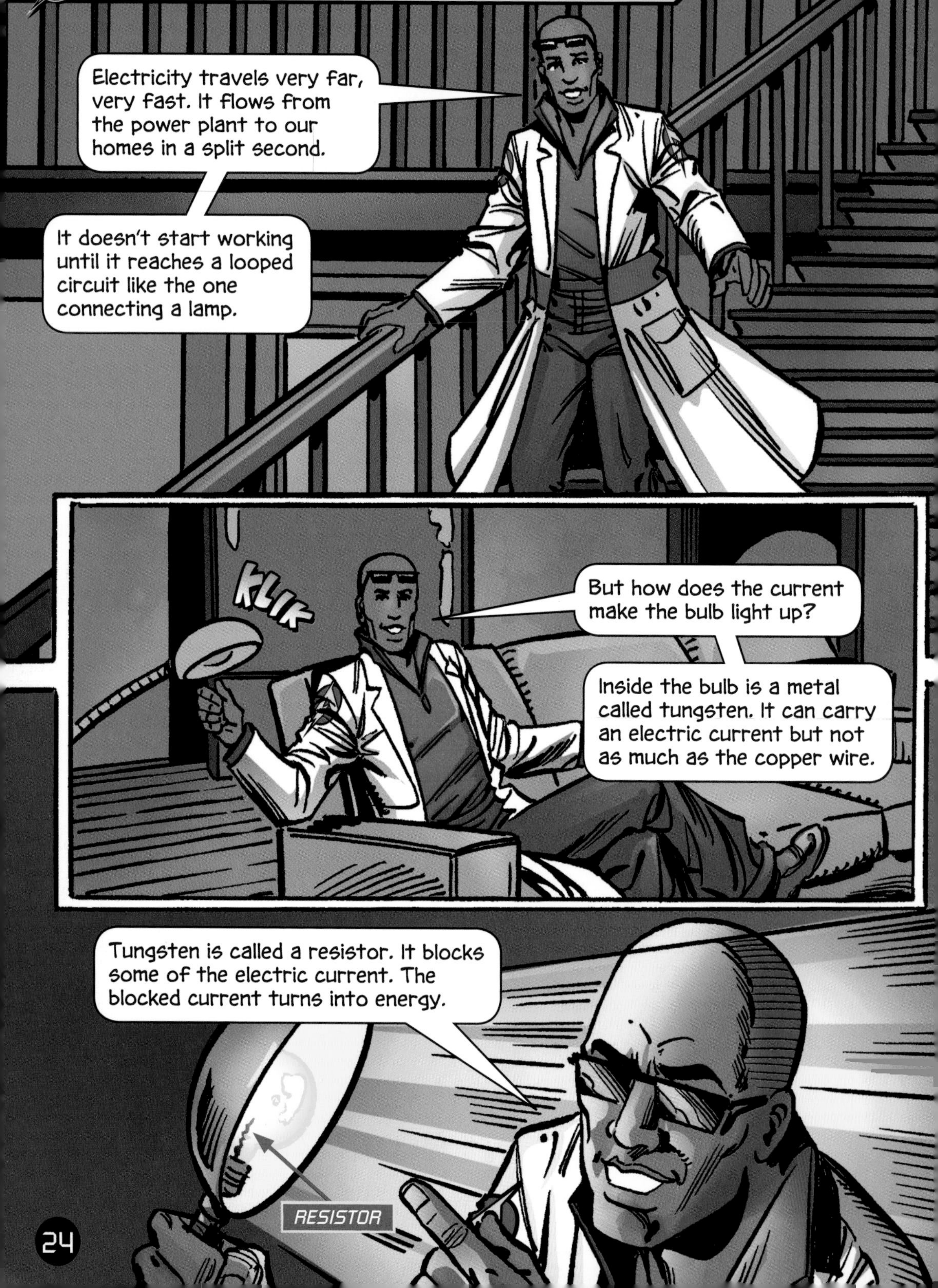
Electricity travels very far, very fast. It flows from the power plant to our homes in a split second.
It doesn't start working until it reaches a looped circuit like the one connecting a lamp.
KLIK
But how does the current make the bulb light up?
Inside the bulb is a metal called tungsten. It can carry an electric current but not as much as the copper wire.
Tungsten is called a resistor. It blocks some of the electric current. The blocked current turns into energy.
RESISTOR

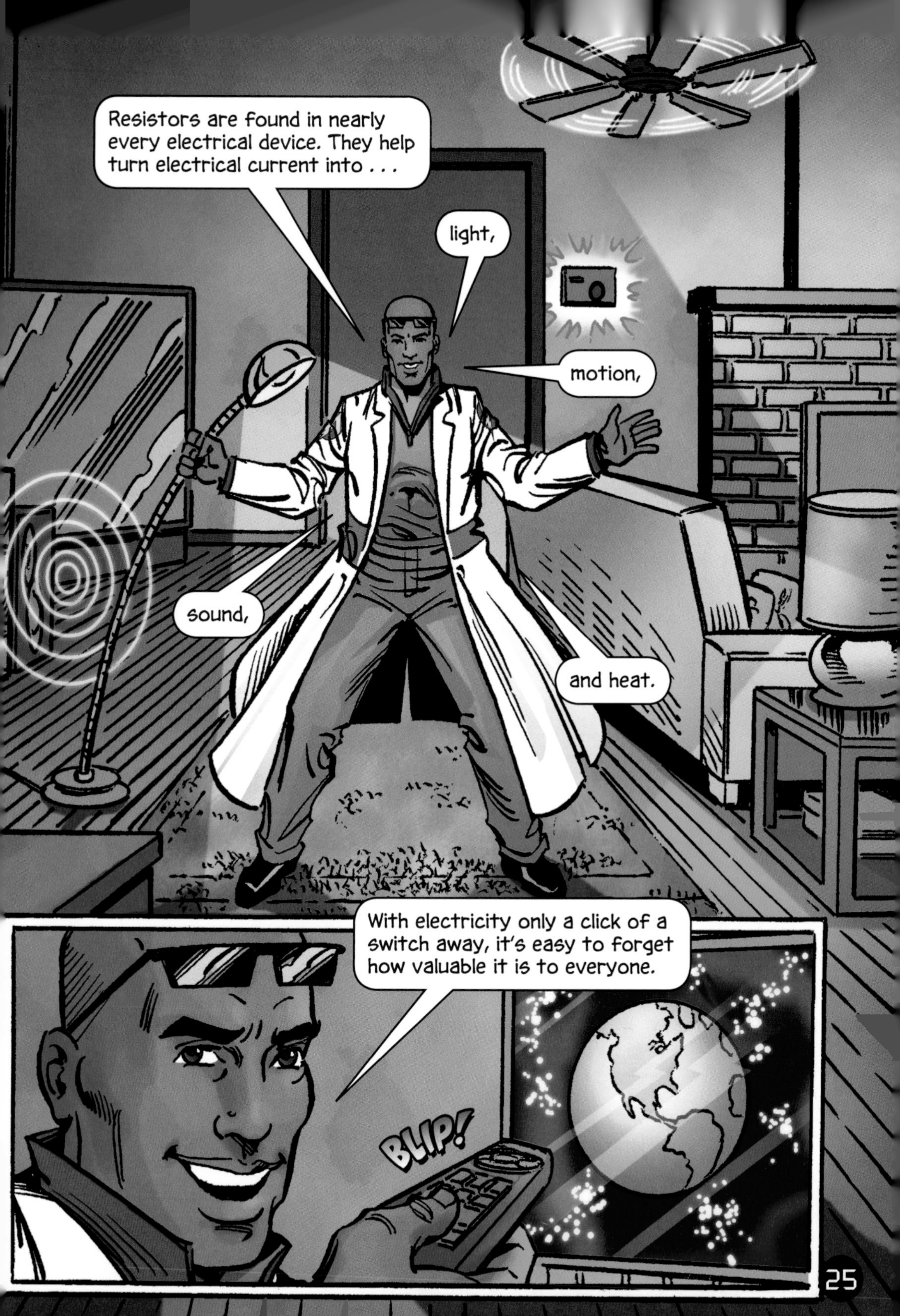
Resistors are found in nearly every electrical device. They help turn electrical current into . . .
light,
motion,
sound,
and heat.
With electricity only a click of a switch away, it's easy to forget how valuable it is to everyone.
BLIP!

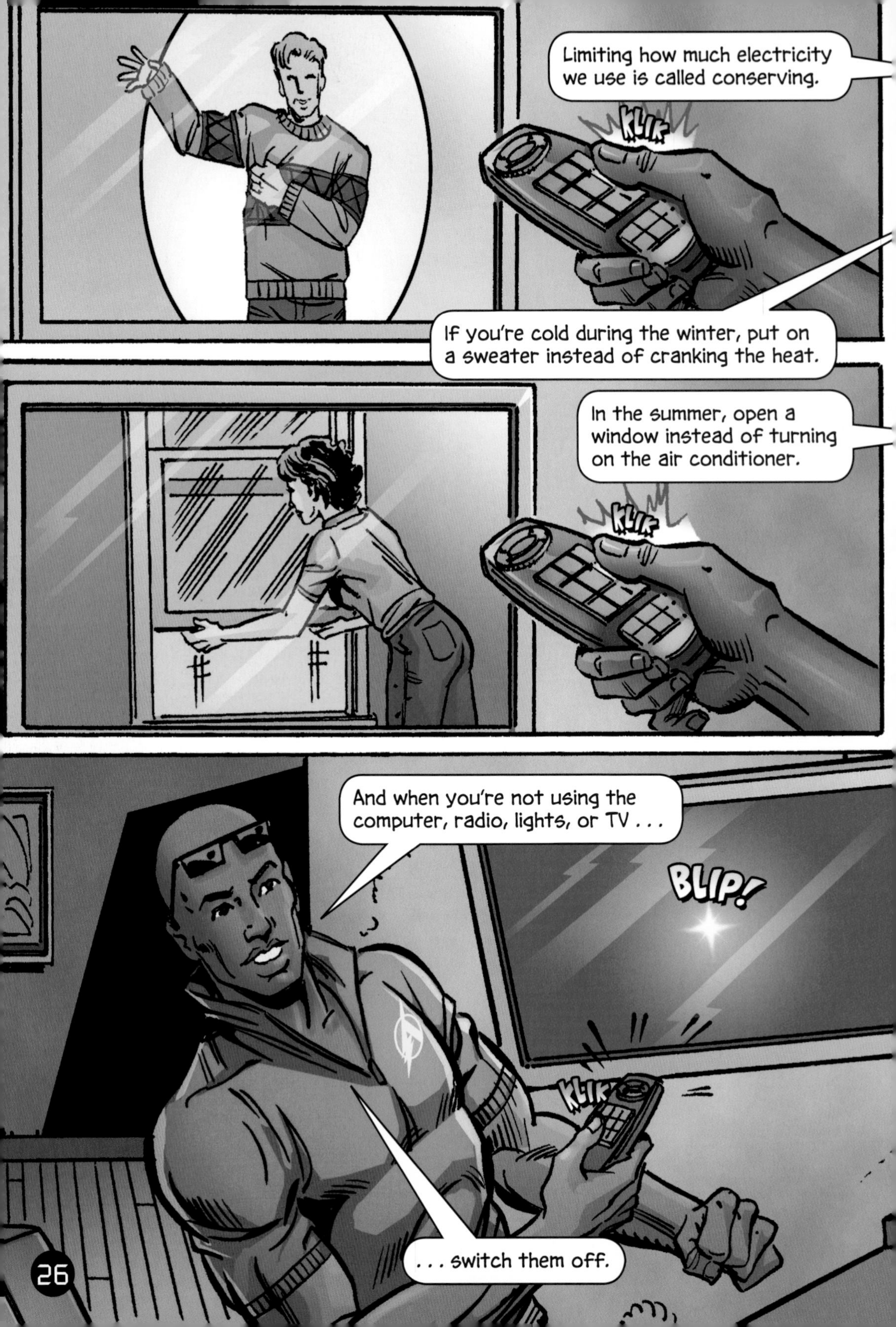

Limiting how much electricity we use is called conserving.
KLIK
If you're cold during the winter, put on a sweater instead of cranking the heat.
In the summer, open a window instead of turning on the air conditioner.
KLIK
And when you're not using the computer, radio, lights, or TV . . .
BLIP!
KLIK
. . . switch them off.

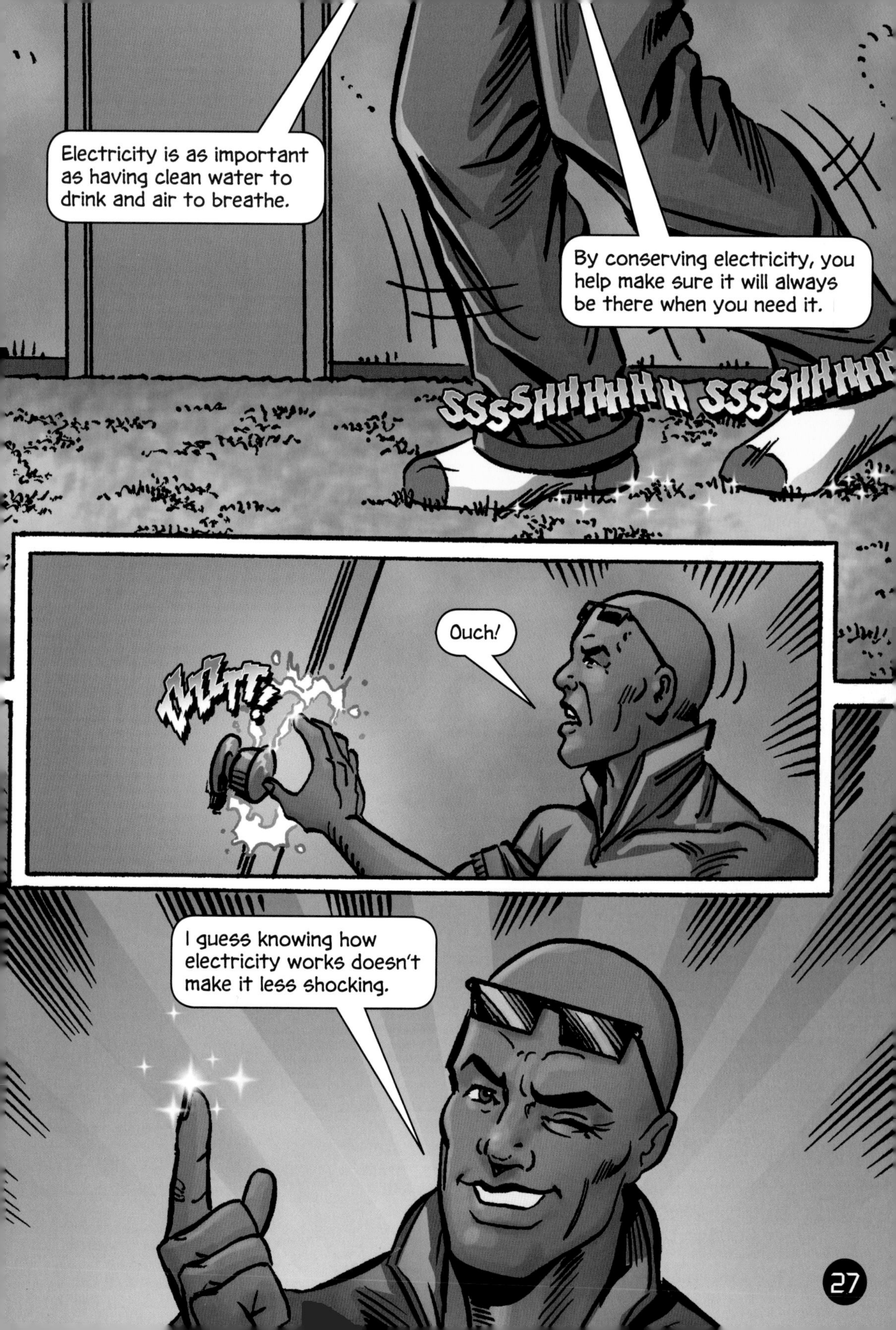
Electricity is as important as having clean water to drink and air to breathe.
By conserving electricity, you help make sure it will always be there when you need it.
SSSSHHHHHH SSSSHHHHH
ZZZTT!
Ouch!
I guess knowing how electricity works doesn't make it less shocking.

ELECTRICITY

In 1752, inventor Benjamin Franklin flew a kite during a thunderstorm to prove that lightning is electricity. As his kite entered a darkened cloud, electricity surged down the string to a key Franklin had attached to the end. When Franklin touched the key, he got a shock. This painful experiment convinced Franklin that lightning and electricity were the same.

In fact, lightning is an extreme form of static electricity. Inside storm clouds, small particles rub together to create a negative electrical charge. This negative electricity stretches down toward positive electricity, which begins rising from the ground. The opposite charges meet to form a brilliant bolt of lightning.

On October 21, 1879, inventor Thomas Edison created an incandescent light bulb. Nearly three years later, he opened the first central power plant in New York City. Soon, thousands of Americans were lighting their homes with Edison's bulbs.

Storms are filled with natural electricity, but sunny skies have energy as well. Solar power is a renewable source of energy from the sun. Specially designed panels called cells capture sunlight and turn it into electricity.

The wires that carry electricity to our homes are extremely dangerous. So, how do birds perch safely on top of them? Electricity always looks for the closest path to the ground. Since birds aren't touching the ground, electricity continues safely along the wires. However, if a person touches the wires while in contact with the ground, he or she could receive a deadly electric shock.

Electricity can also be generated through nuclear fusion. During this process, atoms are smashed together to create an extra electron. The electron creates energy to boil water and turn a turbine. Like solar power, nuclear energy doesn't pollute the air. Unfortunately, it creates dangerous waste.

 Creating electricity often creates pollution, which can be harmful to the environment. To help reduce the amount of electricity used in your home, replace at least one incandescent light bulb with a fluorescent bulb. They can last almost 13 times longer and save electricity. If every U.S. household switched just one bulb, the amount of pollution prevented would compare to taking 1 million cars off the road.

MORE ABOUT

SUPER SCIENTIST

Real name: Maxwell J. Axiom
Hometown: Seattle, Washington
Height: 6' 1"   Weight: 192 lbs
Eyes: Brown   Hair: None

Super capabilities: Super intelligence; able to shrink to the size of an atom; sunglasses give x-ray vision; lab coat allows for travel through time and space.

Origin: Since birth, Max Axiom seemed destined for greatness. His mother, a marine biologist, taught her son about the mysteries of the sea. His father, a nuclear physicist and volunteer park ranger, schooled Max on the wonders of earth and sky.

One day on a wilderness hike, a megacharged lightning bolt struck Max with blinding fury. When he awoke, Max discovered a newfound energy and set out to learn as much about science as possible. He traveled the globe earning degrees in every aspect of the field. Upon his return, he was ready to share his knowledge and new identity with the world. He had become Max Axiom, Super Scientist.

Glossary

amp (AMP)—a unit used to measure the strength of an electrical current

circuit (SUR-kit)—a path for electricity to flow through

conductor (kuhn-DUHK-tur)—a material that lets electricity travel easily through it

current (KUR-uhnt)—a flow of electric charge

electrons (i-LEK-tron)—a tiny particle in an atom that travels around the nucleus

energy (EN-ur-jee)—the ability to move things or do work

generator (JEN-uh-ray-tur)—a machine that makes electricity by turning a magnet inside a coil of wire

insulator (IN-suh-late-ur)—a material that blocks an electrical current

nucleus (NYOO-klee-uhss)—the center of an atom; a nucleus is made up of neutrons and protons.

proton (PRO-tahn)—one of the very small parts in an atom's nucleus

turbine (TUR-bine)—an engine powered by steam or gas; the steam or gas moves through the blades of a fanlike device and makes it turn.

watt (WOT)—a unit for measuring electrical power

READ MORE

Binns, Tristan Boyer. *A Bright Idea: Conserving Energy.* You Can Save the Planet. Chicago: Heinemann, 2005.

Richardson, Adele. *Electricity: A Question and Answer Book.* Fact Finders. Mankato, Minn.: Capstone Press, 2006.

Saunders, Nigel, and Steven Chapman. *Renewable Energy.* Energy Essentials. Chicago: Raintree, 2006.

Stille, Darlene R. *Electricity.* Science Around Us. Chanhassen, Minn.: Child's World, 2005.

Walker, Sally M. *Electricity.* Early Bird Energy. Minneapolis: Lerner, 2006.

INTERNET SITES

FactHound offers a safe, fun way to find Internet sites related to this book. All of the sites on FactHound have been researched by our staff.

Here's how:
1. Visit *www.facthound.com*
2. Choose your grade level.
3. Type in this book ID **0736868356** for age-appropriate sites. You may also browse subjects by clicking on letters, or by clicking on pictures and words.
4. Click on the **Fetch It** button.

FactHound will fetch the best sites for you!

INDEX